WELCOME TO MY COUNTRY

Welcome to the
NETHERLANDS

Gareth Stevens Publishing
A WORLD ALMANAC EDUCATION GROUP COMPANY

Written by
SIMON REYNOLDS/ROSELINE NGCHEONG-LUM

Edited in USA by
DOROTHY L. GIBBS

Designed by
GEOSLYN LIM

Picture research by
SUSAN JANE MANUEL

First published in North America in 2002 by
Gareth Stevens Publishing
A World Almanac Education Group Company
330 West Olive Street, Suite 100
Milwaukee, Wisconsin 53212

Please visit our web site at:
www.garethstevens.com
For a free color catalog describing
Gareth Stevens Publishing's list of high-quality
books and multimedia programs,
call 1-800-542-2595 or
fax your request to (414) 332-3567.

All rights reserved. No parts of this book may be reproduced or utilized in any form or by any means electronic or mechanical, including photocopying, recording, or by an information storage and retrieval system, without permission from the copyright owner.

© **TIMES MEDIA PRIVATE LIMITED 2002**
Originated and designed by
Times Editions
An imprint of Times Media Private Limited
A member of the Times Publishing Group
Times Centre, 1 New Industrial Road
Singapore 536196
http://www.timesone.com.sg/te

Library of Congress Cataloging-in-Publication Data
Reynolds, Simon, 1955-
Welcome to the Netherlands / Simon Reynolds and
Roseline NgCheong-Lum.
p. cm. — (Welcome to my country)
Includes bibliographical references and index.
Contents: Welcome to the Netherlands! — The land — History —
Government and the economy — People and lifestyle — Language —
Arts — Leisure — Food — Map — Quick facts.
ISBN 0-8368-2536-5 (lib. bdg.)
1. Netherlands — Description and travel — Juvenile literature.
2. Netherlands — Social life and customs — Juvenile literature.
[1. Netherlands.] I. NgCheong-Lum, Roseline, 1962- II. Title. III. Series.
DJ18.R49   2002
949.2—dc21   2002017721

Printed in Malaysia

1 2 3 4 5 6 7 8 9 06 05 04 03 02

PICTURE CREDITS
Agence de Presse ANA: 34
Art Directors and Trip Photo Library:
   3 (top), 3 (center), 6, 7, 8, 18, 22,
   26, 35, 37, 38, 40, 45
Downtown MoneyPoint: 44
Victor Englebert: 29
Focus Team — Italy: 4, 41
Robert Fried: 5, 23
Hulton Getty: 10, 11, 12, 15 (top),
   15 (center)
Globe Press: 13, 17
Dave G. Houser: cover, 20 (both), 31,
   33 (bottom)
The Hutchinson Library: 9
Dave Simson: 24, 28, 36, 39
Topham Picturepoint: 1, 2, 3 (bottom),
   14, 15 (bottom), 16, 19, 21, 25, 27, 30,
   32, 43
Travel Ink Photo and Feature Library:
   33 (top)

Digital Scanning by Superskill Graphics Pte Ltd

Contents

Words that appear in the glossary are printed in **boldface** type the first time they occur in the text.

Welcome to the Netherlands!

The Netherlands is a flat country with a lot of water. Besides having many rivers, lakes, and canals, much of the land is below sea level. For centuries, the Dutch have worked to **reclaim** their land from the sea. Let's explore this country of tulips and windmills.

Opposite:
A river and three main canals flow around the center of Amsterdam.

Below: The railroad station in the city of Amsterdam is an important landmark.

The Flag of the Netherlands

The Dutch flag, or **tricolor**, was first used in the early seventeenth century. It has three horizontal bands that, from top to bottom, are red, white, and blue. Queen Wilhelmina named the tricolor the official flag of the Netherlands in 1937.

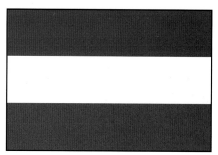

The Land

The land and water of the Netherlands cover an area of 16,033 square miles (41,526 square kilometers). The North Sea is to the north and west. Germany is to the east, and Belgium is south.

The country has twelve provinces. The western provinces of Noord-Holland, Zuid-Holland, and Utrecht are the most well-known and contain most of the Netherlands' big cities.

Left: Although the province of Zuid-Holland is densely populated, it still has country charm.

The southern province of Zeeland is on a **delta** formed by three major rivers, the Rhine, the Schelde, and the Maas. Also in the south, Noord-Brabant is the largest province, and Limburg is the province with the country's highest point, Vaalserberg, which is 1,053 feet (321 meters).

Established in 1986, Flevoland, in the east, is the newest province. It is entirely reclaimed land.

Above: This farm is in Utrecht, but the northern provinces are better areas for farming and have more grazing land.

Climate

The North Sea gives the Netherlands a cool climate. Winter temperatures are rarely below freezing, but strong winds make them seem colder. Summers are cloudy and rainy. The average summer temperature is only 63° Fahrenheit (17° Celsius). Springtime, when all the flowers bloom, is the driest season.

Left: In particularly icy winters, children enjoy skating on Amsterdam's frozen canals and ponds.

Plants and Animals

The Netherlands is famous for its flowers, especially the tulips. Apples, pears, tomatoes, and vegetables also grow well in Dutch soil. Forests grow on only about 8 percent of the land.

With so little forestland, wildlife in the Netherlands is limited. Most of the animals are common mammals, such as squirrels, foxes, and deer, and birds, especially waterbirds such as geese, ducks, and swans.

Above: Farms throughout the Netherlands raise sheep for their wool and meat. Dutch farms also raise dairy cows.

History

People have lived in the Netherlands for about 250,000 years. By 4600 B.C., farming settlements had been started in the area that is now Limburg. In the mid-first century B.C., the Romans took control of the country, except in the north, where the **Frisians** defeated them. In A.D. 407, the **Franks** drove out the Romans, and by 734, they controlled all of the Netherlands.

In 800, Charlemagne (742–814), the king of the Franks, was crowned Holy Roman emperor. The Netherlands was part of his empire. After Charlemagne died, the Franks lost power, and the king of Germany ruled the empire. In the weak German government, bishops and noblemen had the real power, and they divided the Netherlands into small counties. The county of Holland fell to the French dukes of Burgundy in the 1400s. The Netherlands became part of the Holy Roman Empire again in 1504.

Opposite: In this drawing, Frankish warriors of the 300s are fighting for control of the Netherlands.

Below: Under the powerful Frankish king Charlemagne, the Holy Roman Empire stretched from southern Italy to Denmark.

The Provinces Unite

In the 1500s, many Dutch supported a **Protestant** movement against the Roman Catholic Church. Dutch prince William I of Orange helped them fight against Spain's King Philip II, who was Catholic. In 1579, the provinces of Friesland, Gelderland, Groningen, Holland, Overijssel, Utrecht, and Zeeland united to fight for freedom from Spanish rule.

The new Dutch nation **flourished** in the 1600s. Amsterdam became an important European trade center, and the country started colonies in South Africa, Sri Lanka, Indonesia, Brazil, and the West Indies. Dutch art and culture also thrived during this period.

A war with England in the late 1700s weakened the Netherlands, and in 1795, France invaded the country. To keep the French from controlling the Dutch colonies, the Netherlands let Britain **occupy** most of them. The Dutch rebelled against French rule in 1813, and Prince William VI became the first **monarch** of the Kingdom of the Netherlands in 1815.

Left:
This magnificent seventeenth-century building in the city of Amsterdam was the headquarters of the Dutch East India Company.

Queen Wilhelmina's Rule

From 1890 to 1948, Queen Wilhelmina was the Netherlands' monarch. During her reign, the country stayed **neutral** through two world wars. Still, Nazi Germany occupied the nation during most of World War II (1939–1945). Queen Wilhelmina escaped to England but returned in 1945 and established a strong **democratic** government.

Above: Queen Juliana (*right*), the daughter of Queen Wilhelmina, reigned from 1948 to 1980. Her own daughter Princess Beatrix (*left*) is now Queen.

William I of Orange (1533–1584)

A symbol of freedom and **tolerance**, William I led the Protestant revolt against the Spanish army in the 1570s. He was killed by a Catholic in 1584.

William I of Orange

Johan de Witt (1625–1672)

As prime minister from 1653 to 1672, Johan de Witt kept the royal family of Orange out of power. He guided the country through wars with England and Sweden but was killed by his own people when France attacked.

Johan de Witt

Johan Rudolf Thorbecke (1798–1872)

Thorbecke was largely responsible for revising the Dutch constitution, reducing the power of the monarch.

Queen Wilhelmina (1880–1962)

A strong leader, Queen Wilhelmina made radio broadcasts from England to help her country resist the Nazis.

Queen Wilhelmina

Government and the Economy

The king or queen of the Netherlands is the official head of state and signs all laws before they are passed. The prime minister, however, governs the country. The prime minister is appointed by the king or queen. The Dutch parliament, which is called the States-General, has two chambers, or houses. The First

De Europese Raad
vergaderde in het Gouvernement
op 9 en 10 december 1991
Het Verdrag van Maastricht
werd hier getekend
op 7 februari 1992

Chamber has seventy-five members elected by the local governments of the country's twelve provinces. The Second Chamber has 150 members elected by the people. A provincial council and a commissioner, who is appointed by the monarch, run the local government in each province.

Armed forces in the Netherlands, which include an army, a navy, an air force, and military police, guard the nation's borders and the royal palaces.

The Economy

The Netherlands is a small country, yet it is the world's third largest exporter of agricultural products. These exports include tomatoes, cucumbers, lettuce, butter, and cheese.

While half of the country's land is used for farming, only 4 percent of the workforce have agricultural jobs. The family-run farms are small, but they use modern machinery and chemical fertilizers for high output.

Left: Hyacinths are one of many kinds of flowers Dutch farmers grow. Like tulips and daffodils, hyacinths grow from bulbs.

Manufacturing and trade also are very important to the economy of the Netherlands. Shipbuilding is a major industry, along with the production of metals, chemicals, textiles, and rubber.

Because of where it is located, the Netherlands is an international trade center. More than a third of all goods shipped to countries in the European Union passes through its ports.

Above: The World Trade Center, which is in Rotterdam, is really two buildings. The lower building was constructed over sixty years ago. The tower on top of it was built in 1986.

People and Lifestyle

One of the best characteristics of the Dutch is their tolerance of people's differences. About 60,000 **immigrants** come into the country each year. In the past, most came from Dutch colonies, such as Indonesia. Today, more are coming from European nations.

Above: Dutch people often wear traditional clothing on Sundays and for special occasions, but some dress in traditional outfits every day.

Left: Most Dutch are descendants of German groups, such as the Franks, and most of them have fair skin, blue eyes, and blond hair.

The Dutch live mainly in cities and towns. They are proud of their homes and keep them neat and clean. In the cities, most people live in town houses or apartments. In the towns, families live in houses with flower gardens.

City people usually work five days a week and keep weekends for family and leisure activities. In the country, farmers start work at dawn and take their crops to weekly village markets.

Family Life

Most Dutch families are small, with only two or three children. Older adults live in their own homes, but they often see their children and grandchildren on weekends. Eating meals together is important in Dutch families. Parents and children usually eat breakfast and dinner together, and they eat lunch together, too, if they can.

Below:
This happy couple is celebrating their wedding outside the town hall in Veere, Zeeland.

Women and Children

By law, Dutch women have the same rights as men, but they still earn less money than men for doing the same work. Most Dutch women, however, prefer to be mothers and homemakers. Less than half of the mothers work, and most of those have only part-time jobs. Dutch parents are very loving and allow their children to have a voice in many family decisions.

Above:
Young women in the Netherlands are free to choose any lifestyle they like.

Education

The Netherlands has one of the best education systems in the world, so the country's **literacy** rate is very high. All children between the ages of five and sixteen must attend school. Education is free, even though most schools are run by private organizations.

From ages five to twelve, children attend elementary school. Then they go on to one of four types of high schools, which prepare them either for work or for more education at a university.

Above:
After elementary school, most Dutch students go to junior general high school for four years. Dutch students preparing for college, however, attend high school for six years.

Eight of the Netherlands' thirteen universities are run by the government. The oldest is Leiden University, which was founded in 1575. The newest is the Open University, founded in 1984.

The Netherlands has eighty-five more institutions for higher learning, called polytechnics. These schools teach students a **vocation** or trade, along with related academic subjects.

Below: Utrecht University, which was founded in 1636, is the third oldest university in the Netherlands.

Religion

All major religions of the world can be found in the Netherlands, but the main religion is Christianity. Most people in the northern part of the country are Protestant Christians. In the southern

Left:
Catholic churches in the Netherlands are usually designed with many decorative architectural details. Protestant churches have a plainer look.

Left: This mosque in Amsterdam is a place of worship for Muslims, who are people of the Islamic faith.

Netherlands, most people are Roman Catholics. Dutch Catholics, however, outnumber Protestants overall. Dutch Protestants belong mainly to one of two churches of the Calvinist faith.

About 3 percent of the population are Muslims. Most Dutch Muslims are immigrants from Indonesia, Morocco, and Turkey. The Netherlands also has Buddhists, Hindus, and Jews.

Language

Dutch is a guttural language, which means that the sounds are made far back in the throat. In print, Dutch is the same all over the country, but it is spoken differently in different regions. In many ways, the Dutch language is like German and English. In Friesland, people speak Frisian, a language that is more closely related to English than to Dutch.

Left: This woman in Limburg is reading *de Volkskrant*, one of Amsterdam's daily newspapers.

Literature

Among modern Dutch writers, Simon Carmiggelt (1913–1987) is probably the most famous. He is best known for the humorous short stories about life that he wrote for a daily newspaper.

Women authors in the Netherlands have had their works published since at least the twelfth century. The first woman writer was Hadewijch. Two twentieth-century women writers are Marga Minco and Maria Stahlie.

Above: The Dutch like to read. The literacy rate in the Netherlands has been at 99 percent since 1979.

29

Arts

Painting

Seventeenth-century Dutch paintings are world treasures. *Sunflower*, painted by Rembrandt (1606–1669), is one of that era's masterpieces. Vincent van Gogh (1853–1890) is a world-famous Dutch artist of the **Impressionist** era.

Left: Dutch artist Jan Vermeer (1632–1675) is known for painting female figures such as this 1665 portrait.

Music

The Dutch love music, and almost every family has at least one member who can play an instrument. Dutch musicians were among the first who used early instruments to play modern music. Today, the Amsterdam Baroque Orchestra is world-famous for this kind of performance. Amsterdam's Royal Concertgebouw Qrchestra is, however, the most well-known Dutch orchestra.

Architecture

In the Middle Ages, the most popular Dutch architecture was **Gothic**. In the seventeenth century, however, due to limited space in Dutch cities, new laws allowed houses to be only as wide as three windows. Most houses then were tall and narrow. While windmills have become a symbol of the Netherlands, the Dutch did not invent them.

Furniture and Other Crafts

Sixteenth-century Dutch furniture is known for its solid construction and its **intricate** carvings. In the early days of Dutch trade with countries in the **Far East**, **lacquered** furniture became popular. It is still preferred by people on the Wadden Islands. Many Dutch homes have big Frisian clocks, which have been popular since the 1600s.

Above: Pottery is made throughout the Netherlands, but some of the finest porcelain in the world is made in Delft.

Pottery, wooden shoes, and lace are traditional Dutch crafts still being made in villages and small towns.

Left: Dutch farmers wear wooden shoes every day, but they are not the same as the mass-produced wooden shoes sold to tourists.

Leisure

Dutch people spend much of their free time at home. Gardening is a favorite hobby. Families who live in apartments will even rent small plots of land so they can grow flowers and vegetables. In winter, the Dutch enjoy cozy chats by the fireside. They also like to read and listen to music.

Left: The Dutch will grow their flowers and other plants almost anywhere.

Left:
A sidewalk café is one of the places where Dutch people go to meet friends or relax with a cup of coffee. These outdoor cafés can be found in most Dutch cities.

"Brown" and "White" Cafés

Cafés are part of the Dutch lifestyle. Older people like to visit brown cafés. These coffeehouses are called "brown" because their walls are stained from tobacco smoke. Brown cafés are like living rooms, with comfortable chairs and books and magazines all around. Young people prefer "white" cafés, which have a more modern design and lots of light and open space.

Soccer

The Dutch are big soccer fans. In the 1970s, the Dutch national soccer team proved to be one of the best in the world. It reached the finals of the World Cup in both 1974 and 1978.

More recently, the final matches of the Euro 2000 soccer championships were held in Rotterdam.

Above: The Dutch came out in huge numbers to support their national soccer team at the Euro 2000 championships.

Other Sports

Because the Netherlands is so flat, walking and cycling are popular activities. Dutch cyclists regularly compete in the Tour de France cycling event, and the Nijmegen marathon is a popular four-day challenge for walkers.

Water sports are popular, too, even in winter, when frozen lakes and canals become skating rinks. *Elfstedentocht* (elf-STAY-den-tokt) is an ice-skating competition in Friesland that is held only when all of the canals are frozen.

Left: Windsurfing is a popular summer water sport in the Netherlands. Dutch people also enjoy swimming, sailing, and water skiing.

Festivals

Carnaval is a festival that is celebrated throughout the Netherlands forty days before Easter. On the Monday before Carnaval, children put on fancy clothes and search the town for the Carnaval Prince, who is dressed up in a costume. The festival features processions, giant puppets, and colorful floats. People, young and old, wear masks and parade through the streets, playing music and singing. The end of Carnaval marks the beginning of **Lent**.

On April 30, the Dutch celebrate Queensday. This public holiday is the **official birthday** of the Dutch queen. On this day, the queen always wears orange, which represents the House of Orange, and visits a different town each year. People crowd the streets to see her, while musicians and acrobats entertain them. Queensday is the only day the Dutch can sell whatever they like without a license, so the whole country becomes a street market.

Opposite: Carnaval participants often dress up in elaborate costumes to make the festival even more colorful.

Below: This float made of flowers is part of a parade from Aalsmeer to Amsterdam for the September flower festival. The city of Aalsmeer has the world's largest flower market.

Food

Dutch food used to be heavy and high in fat. Today, Dutch dishes have less animal fat and include more fruits and vegetables. Each Dutch province has special dishes made from the products grown or raised there. People in the north raise cattle, chickens, and pigs, so they eat a lot of meat. Restaurants in Zeeland serve a lot of seafood, such as mussels, oysters, and sole.

Below: Most Dutch people like simple, hearty meals that usually include meat or fish and vegetables.

Left: Many dishes in towns along the southwestern coast of the Netherlands include fish or some other seafood.

Thick soups, mashed vegetables, and herring are favorite traditional foods. Green-pea soup is very popular. Smoked sausage and cabbage mashed with potatoes is a traditional winter dish. Herring, either raw or cooked, is usually eaten as a snack.

Popular Dutch desserts include *Boterletter* (boh-ter-LET-ter), a puff pastry with almond filling. Coffee is the country's favorite drink. Even children drink it, hot or cold, usually mixed with a little chocolate milk.

A   **B**   **C**   **D**

	Province Boundary
■	Capital
●	City
	River
⊢⊣	Dam

1

WADDEN ISLANDS

Wadden Sea

GRONINGEN

●Groningen

FRIESLAND

DRENTHE

N O R T H

2

S E A

NOORD-HOLLAND

FLEVOLAND

OVERIJSSEL

AMSTERDAM■

Amstel

3

N

●Aalsmeer

RANDSTAD

●Leiden

UTRECHT

GELDERLAND

IJssel

ZUID-HOLLAND

The Hague●

Delft●

Lower Rhine

●Rotterdam

Waal

●Nijmegen

Rhine

Maas

NOORD-BRABANT

GERMANY

4

Veere●

East Schelde

West Schelde

ZEELAND

LIMBURG

BELGIUM

Schelde

5

THE NETHERLANDS

●Maastricht

▲*Vaalserberg*
(1,053 ft / 321 m)

42

Above: These huge wooden shoes were not made for walking.

Aalsmeer B3
Amstel (river) B3
Amsterdam B3

Belgium A5–C5

Delft B3
Drenthe C2–D2

East Schelde A4

Flevoland C2–C3
Friesland C1–D2

Gelderland C3–D4
Germany D1–C5
Groningen (city) D1
Groningen
     (province) C1–D2

Hague, The B3

IJssel (river) C2–C3

Leiden B3
Limburg C4–C5

Maas (river) B4–C5
Maastricht C5

Nijmegen C4
Noord-Brabant
     B4–C4
Noord-Holland
     B2–B3
North Sea A4–D1

Overijssel C2–D3

Randstad
     (region) B3

Rhine (river) A3–D5
Rotterdam B4

Schelde (river)
     A4–B5

Utrecht B3–C3

Vaalserberg C5
Veere A4

Waal (river) A3–C4
Wadden Islands
     B2–D1
Wadden Sea B2–C1
West Schelde A4

Zeeland A4–A5
Zuid-Holland
     A4–B3

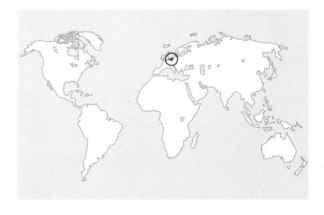

43

Quick Facts

Official Name	Kingdom of the Netherlands
Capital	Amsterdam
Official Language	Dutch
Population	15.9 million (July 2001 estimate)
Land Area	16,033 square miles (41,526 square km)
Provinces	Drenthe, Flevoland, Friesland, Gelderland, Groningen, Limburg, Noord-Brabant, Noord-Holland, Overijssel, Utrecht, Zeeland, Zuid-Holland.
Highest Point	Vaalserberg (1,053 feet/321 m)
Major Rivers	IJessel, Maas, Rhine, Schelde, Waal
Major Religion	Christian (Roman Catholic and Protestant)
National Flower	Tulip
Holidays	New Year's Day (January 1) Carnaval (February/March) Queensday (April 30) National Windmill Day (May) Sinterklaas (December 5)
Currency	Euro (EUR 1.16 = U.S. $1 as of 2002)

Opposite: These men are carrying cheese that has just been weighed.

Glossary

delta: a flat, triangle-shaped area of land that is formed by deposits of sand and soil at the mouth of a river.

democratic: related to a political system in which people rule themselves by electing representatives to make laws and run the government.

Dutch East India Company: a major shipping business in the Netherlands that controlled most of the Dutch trade with the Far East in the 1600s and the 1700s.

Far East: the countries of eastern and southeastern Asia, such as China, Japan, Korea, and Indonesia.

flourished: grew to be strong, healthy, and successful.

Franks: an ancient German tribe that settled along the Rhine River.

Frisians: the people who live in the Netherlands province of Friesland.

Gothic: a style of architecture in the Middle Ages that featured tall stone frameworks and pointed arches.

immigrants: people who move from their home countries to live permanently in other countries.

Impressionist: a style of painting in the late 1800s that used strokes and dabs of color to imitate the effects of natural light and give objects a natural appearance.

intricate: having a lot of details.

lacquered: coated with a varnishlike liquid that dries to form a smooth, hard, shiny finish.

Lent: the Christian season of fasting during the forty days before Easter.

literacy: being able to read and write.

monarch: the king, queen, or other ruler of a kingdom or an empire.

neutral: not taking part or helping either side in a dispute such as a war.

occupy: take over or capture another country's territory.

official birthday: the day of celebration established by a government or some other authority.

Protestant: related to all Christian religions, except Catholic.

reclaim: take back for human use by changing unsuitable or undesirable natural conditions.

tolerance: respecting beliefs and ways of life that are different from our own.

tricolor: a flag that is divided into three equal parts, and each part is a different color.

vocation: a profession or a specialized line of work in which a person is or hopes to be employed.

More Books to Read

Amsterdam. Cities of the World series. Deborah Kent (Children's Press)

A Day on Skates. Hilda van Stockum (Bethlehem Books)

Hiding from the Nazis. David A. Adler (Holiday House)

Katje the Windmill Cat. Gretchen Woelfle (Candlewick Press)

The Netherlands. Countries of the World series. Michael S. Dahl (Bridgestone Books)

Netherlands. Festivals of the World series. Joyce van Fenema (Gareth Stevens)

A Picture Book of Anne Frank. David A. Adler (Live Oak Media)

Tulips. Flowers series. John F. Prevost (Abdo & Daughters)

Vincent van Gogh: Sunflowers and Swirly Stars. Smart about Art series. Brad Bucks and Joan Holub (Grosset & Dunlap)

Videos

Beautiful Cities of the World: Amsterdam. (Madacy Entertainment)

Cycling Central Holland. (eurocycle.com)

Hidden Treasures of Europe: Holland. (BFS Entertainment & Multimedia)

Tulip: Treasure of Springtime. (Jim Waldsmith's Creative Arts)

Web Sites

travelforkids.com/Funtodo/Netherlands/netherlands.htm

www.geocities.com/Paris/Metro/2954/

www.homepages.hetnet.nl/~posnv/

www.xs4all.nl/~eleede/

Due to the dynamic nature of the Internet, some web sites stay current longer than others. To find additional web sites, use a reliable search engine with one or more of the following keywords to help you locate information about the Netherlands: *Amsterdam, Delft, Holland, tulips, van Gogh, windmills, wooden shoes.*

Index